I made this book to show how much I love you!

To ____________

From ____________

My dad looks like this :

Our favorite thing to do together is

You are super awesome because you

____

____

____

____

The best thing about you is

You always smile when

A poem about my dad

You are the happiest when

You are there for me when

My favorite memory of us

You taught me how to

We all had so much fun when we went to

I like it when you tell me that I am

____

____

____

____

Four words describe You

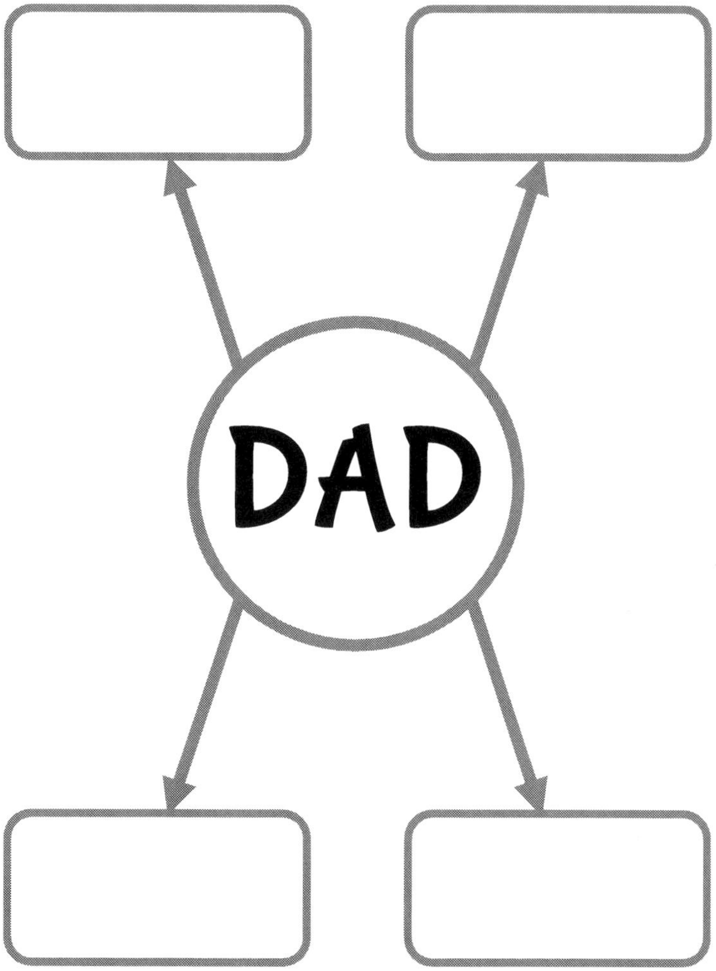

You make me laugh when

The funniest thing you do is

BEST
DAD
EVER
YOU ARE THE KING

You always help me to

You are good at

You are smarter than

Your favorite food is

Movie/TV show that we both love is

I enjoyed
a lot when we
went to

I love you because

I'm proud to say you are

Made in United States
Orlando, FL
04 December 2022

25485823R00024